Feasts and Festivals

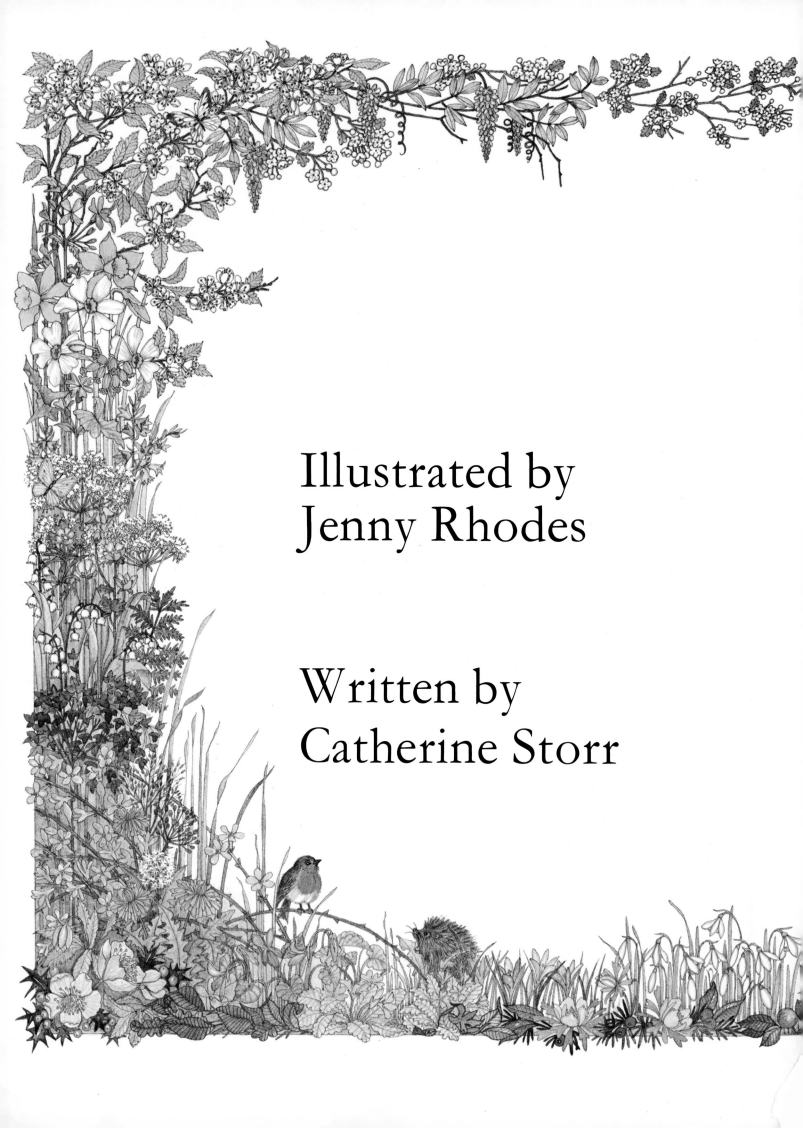

Illustrated by
Jenny Rhodes

Written by
Catherine Storr

FEASTS AND FESTIVALS

Patrick Hardy Books
1983

To Frank, and to my silent partner, Bobby.

First published in 1983
by PATRICK HARDY BOOKS
28 Percy Street
London W1P 9FF

Produced by:
Belitha Press Ltd.,
40 Belitha Villas, London, N1 1PD

Illustrations © Jenny Rhodes 1983
Text © Catherine Storr 1983
© in this format Belitha Press Ltd. 1983

ISBN 0 7444 0000 7

Printed in Great Britain
by W. S. Cowell Ltd., 8 Butter Market,
Ipswich, Suffolk

Contents

January: *Twelfth Night*   7

                Up-Helly-Aa   8

February: *Candlemas*   10

                St. Valentine's Day   11

                Shrove Tuesday   12

March: *St. Patrick's Day*   14

                Oranges and Lemons   15

April: *April Fool's Day*   16

                Palm Sunday   17

                Easter   18

                St. George's Day   19

May: *May Dawn*   20

                May Day   21

                Furry Dance   22

June: *Lady Godiva*   23

               Midsummer's Eve   24

July: *St. Swithin's Day*   26

               St. James's Grotto Day   27

               Swan-Upping   28

August: *Clipping the Church*   30

               Plague Sunday   31

September: *Harvest Home*   32

               Horn Dance   34

October: *The Bellringers' Feast*   35

               Goose Fair   36

               Souling   37

               Hallowe'en   38

November: *Bonfire Night*   40

               Martinmas   41

December: *St. Nicholas's Day*   42

               Christmas Eve   43

               Christmas Day   45

               New Year's Eve   46

               Epilogue   47

               Picture Sources   48

January

Twelfth Night

January 6 is Twelfth Night. It is the last of the twelve hallowed days of Christmas. Farmers used to go into their orchards to wassail their trees with:

> *Apple tree, apple tree,*
> *Bear apples for me,*
> *Hats full, laps full,*
> *Sacks full, caps full,*
> *Apple tree, apple tree,*
> *Bear apples for me.*

Up-Helly-Aa

At the end of January, in the Shetland Islands, far to the north of Britain, an ancient Viking tradition is honoured. A torchlight procession, led by a dragon-headed Norse galley,

winds through the town of Lerwick
to the sea front. Here the
Norsemen leave their ship,
and the torch bearers
throw their flaming
torches at it till
it disappears
in a blaze
of fire.

9

February

Candlemas

February 2 is Candlemas Day. People used to bring candles to
the church to be blessed, and then carried them in procession,
in thankfulness for the gift of light.

The last bit of Christmas greenery was taken down by this
day, for fear of the goblins who would hide there. Now we
do this on January 6, Twelfth Night.

St. Valentine's Day

February 14. Valentine is the saint of lovers. On his name day, birds choose their mates, and young men and girls exchange love gifts. The gift may be a card, a loving message, a posy of flowers, or a pair of gloves – sent without the giver's name. The loved one has to guess who has sent them and who this year's sweetheart may be.

Shrove Tuesday

Shrove Tuesday is the last day before Lent, the six lean weeks before Easter, when Christian people remember the forty days Jesus spent in the wilderness. Many people give up eating meat and other good things during Lent. So Shrove Tuesday is the last day for feasting and dancing.

Eggs will take the place of meat from now on, so this is Pancake Day, when the women of Olney run in the pancake race. This starts in the market square and ends at the church door, and as the women run they have to toss a pancake three times in the pan.

March

St. Patrick's Day

March 17. St. Patrick is the patron saint of Ireland, and on this day every true Irish man and woman likes to wear the three-leaved shamrock in his honour. St. Patrick's best known miracle was to banish all poisonous snakes from Ireland. He forced them all to go to the top of a high cliff, from which he made them swarm over the edge into the sea below, where they were drowned. Some people say that one old serpent would not obey. St. Patrick made a box, and invited the serpent to get into it. The old serpent said the box was too small, and to prove this, he got into the box, on which St. Patrick slammed down the lid, and threw the box into the sea.

Oranges and Lemons

March 31. In the days when the River Thames at London was wider than it is now, barges carrying oranges and lemons landed just below the churchyard of St. Clement Dane. On the last day of March, children gathered at the church to attend a service and to receive presents of fruit. The tune of "Oranges and Lemons" is still played on the church bells of St. Clement Dane.

April

April Fool's Day

April 1. On this morning people try to trick their friends, to make them behave like fools. One tells another that his shoe is unbuckled or that there is a spider in his hair. A boy is sent to buy a pot of striped paint or a pig with a straight tail. When the victim tries to buckle his shoe or to brush the spider from his hair, or goes to look for the paint or the pig, the joker cries out, "April Fool!"

Palm Sunday

On Palm Sunday, a week before Easter, Christians
remember how Jesus rode into Jerusalem
on a donkey. People laid palm branches on
the ground in front of him. On
this Sunday before Easter the
churches are often decorated
with palms or
pussy willows.

Easter

If you go out before dawn on Easter Sunday, you may be lucky enough to see the sun dance for joy, leaping up and down, and changing colour. On this day nearly two thousand years ago Jesus arose from the dead, and since then people have celebrated Easter with gladness.

At breakfast, the boiled eggs are coloured or have painted faces, and the Easter Hare has hidden more eggs around the house. Egg-Rolling is an Easter game. Hard boiled eggs are rolled down hill, and the person whose egg rolls longest without cracking becomes the Easter champion.

Many people have new clothes to wear on Easter Day.

St. George's Day

April 23 is the day of St. George, the patron saint of England. The legend tells us that St. George killed a terrible dragon which had been devastating the countryside, and some say that this won him the hand of a beautiful princess.

St. George's symbol is the English rose.

May

May 1. The night before the first of May is a time when the doors between fairyland and our world are opened. This is when the fairies are on the watch for human babies to steal, or pipe players and fiddlers to entice into their fairy hills to play for dancing. The girls search for May morning dew to wash their faces and make them beautiful.

May Day

On the village green the tall Maypole is set up, and the school children deck it with ribbons and flowers, while others dress the May garland and carry it round from house to house. When everyone has seen it, the May Queen and the May King dance with the other boys and girls around the Maypole, weaving its ribbons into patterns as they cross and pass each other.

Furry Dance

May 8. Long ago, in France, the Archangel Michael fought long and hard with the Devil. At last he escaped from him across the English Channel to Cornwall. The Devil hurled after him an enormous lump of granite, which missed the Archangel, but fell into the village of Helston, where it can still be seen. To celebrate this and to welcome the summer, the villagers of Helston dance right through the village, in and out of all the houses, wearing their best clothes and carrying lilies of the valley, while they sing:

For Summer is a-come, O!
And Winter is a-gone, O!

June

Lady Godiva

Nine hundred years ago, Leofric, Earl of Mercia, promised his wife that he would take less money from the poor people of Coventry if she would ride naked through the city, thinking she would not dare. But Godiva was so sorry for the people that she rode on a white horse through the streets, covered only by her long hair. The people were grateful, and went into their houses shutting the doors and windows. No one looked, except Peeping Tom, and for his curiosity God struck him blind.

Today, Godiva's ride is remembered again in the Coventry Show Fair.

June 23. People used to believe that this was the most magical night of the whole year, when humans might see sights hidden from them on every other night. They might see fairies and spirits. They might see the Wild Hunt rushing through forests, or in the air above; men and women, with hunting dogs and horns and fiery horses.

On this night, humans could work magic too. They could cure poor sight with the night's dew, or make themselves invisible by plucking fern seed at midnight. Bonfires were lit on the beacon hills of the West country, to celebrate the defeat of the great Spanish Armada, four hundred years ago. Boys and girls leapt over the burning ashes for luck.

At Stonehenge the summer solstice is celebrated, as the sun, standing still in his glory at the height of summer, strikes on the sun stone, at dawn on Midsummer's Day.

Midsummer's Eve

July

St. Swithin's Day

In July, when the hay is cut and turned
in the fields, and piled into haycocks,
everyone hopes that the sun will shine
and that the hay harvest can be gathered
in, dry and sweet.

But if there is rain on **July 15,** the day
of St. Swithin, they say there will be
forty more days of wet weather. So the
wise farmer gets his hay-crop cut and
stacked early, before this day.

St. James's Grotto Day

July 25. After St. James had died in Jerusalem, his body was brought by boat back to Spain. A man rode his horse into the sea to welcome the saint's return and would have been drowned, if the dead saint had not rescued him by a miracle. As they came out from the sea, the rider and his horse were seen to be covered with scallop shells, and so these shells became the emblem of St. James, the patron of all pilgrims.

To celebrate St. James's Day, children used to make little grottoes from moss and flowers and shells; scallop shells if they could get them, but if not, oyster shells, while they sang:

Please to remember the Grotto
It's only once a year.

Swan-Upping

All the swans on the River Thames belong to the Queen
of England and two Companies, the Vintners and the
Dyers. **On a Monday in July,** the Queen's Swanherd
meets the two Swan Wardens of the Companies at
Southwark Bridge in London. A procession of six skiffs
goes up the river as far as Henley-on-Thames, to find and
mark all the cygnets hatched this year.

First comes the Queen's Swan Keeper in scarlet livery,
next comes the Vintner's Swan Master in green livery and
last comes the Dyer's Swan Master in blue livery.

August

Clipping the Church

August. In different parts of the country, at different times of the year, children take part in the ceremony of Clipping the Church. In Guiseley, Yorkshire, this happens on **August 5**. The village band plays as it circles round the church, then all the village children, dressed in their best clothes, join hands and make a huge circle right around the church. As they sing the Clipping Hymn, they surge forwards towards the church, then retreat. When they have done this three times, the church has been properly "clipped" for the coming year.

Plague Sunday

August. In 1665, people in Derbyshire must have felt safe
from the Great Plague then raging in London, more than a
hundred miles away. But a bundle of cloth, sent from London
to the tailor of the little village of Eyam, brought the terrible
disease with it, and more than half the villagers caught it and
died. Their Rector persuaded the people not to run away and
spread the plague. He arranged for food to be brought from
nearby villages and left on a stone by a spring where the
Eyam villagers could collect it.

Today, on **the last Sunday of August,** the villagers hold
a service to remember their ancestors and the Rector.

Harvest Home

September. When the ripe golden corn was at last cut, everyone joined in rejoicing over a successful harvest. The last load was brought home in triumph, piled high on a wagon decorated with flowers and branches of oak and ash, and drawn by a team of garlanded horses. The harvesters rode on top of the load, shouting and singing and blowing horns.

September

The last sheaf of corn to be cut was made into the Corn Dolly. This was kept in the farmhouse for the coming year, for it held the spirit of the corn. The day ended with a huge feast, and everyone drank the health of the farmer, his wife and family, while *they* drank the health of the harvesters.

Horn Dance

On a Monday morning in early September, twelve men of Abbots Bromley in Staffordshire go to the parish church to collect six pairs of reindeer horns with which they will perform the Horn Dance.

The six principal dancers carry the huge horns on their heads. The others take the parts of Robin Hood, Maid Marian, the Hobby, the Fool, the Musician and a Boy with a triangle. The dance is first performed on the village green and then in front of every farm, great house and hamlet nearby.

October

The Bellringers' Feast

October. As the nights became longer, travellers used to lose their way on country roads. So, in different villages, from North to South, from East to West, the "Lost-in-the-Dark" bell was rung in the churches to guide wayfarers safely home.

A Bellringers' Feast was given when the nightly ringing began in the Autumn and another when it was no longer needed in the Spring.

Goose Fair

October. Across the country flocks of geese
used to be driven towards Nottingham for the great
Goose Fair. Sometimes kind cobblers made little slippers
of soft leather to protect the feet of the weary geese on
their long march.

Goose Fair was also a hiring fair, where workers on
the land looked for next year's masters. After bargaining
for good wages all the morning, the reapers, the
cowherds and the dairymaids spent the afternoon eating
gingerbread and frumenty, and seeing all the sights of the
fair.

Souling

October 31. On All Souls' Eve, children went round to their neighbours' houses, singing:

Remember the departed,
for holy Mary's sake,
And of your charity, pray,
give us a big soul cake.

Today they may call out, "Trick or Treat!" If they are not given a soul cake—a little round spicy bun—or an apple, a few coins or sweets, they will play tricks.

Hallowe'en

October 31. This same night everyone should be wary. Not only the gentle souls are around, for tonight the Fairy Court rides abroad. Witches, ghosts and goblins are free to infest the darkness. Bonfires are lit to scare them away, and, as everyone knows, a sprig of rowan or hazel on the house door will keep them out.

In some places they used to say that on this night wayfarers would find a little black sow with a ring through her tail at every stile. Later there are great parties, with games to see who is cleverest at apple-bobbing and ducking for money. After midnight the spirits can foretell the future, and girls brushing their hair before the mirror may see the faces of their true loves looking over their shoulders.

November

Bonfire Night

November 5. This is the anniversary of the day, nearly four hundred years ago, when a man called Guy Fawkes plotted with four friends to blow up the Houses of Parliament while the King was there. The plot was discovered in time, and the five conspirators caught and punished.

On this day children make "guys" out of straw and old clothes which they show to passers-by on the street and then burn on huge bonfires, while a great show of fireworks lights up the dark winter sky.

Martinmas

November 11. We remember St. Martin, the patron of the wheel. His feast day used to be a holiday for carters, millers and spinning women, who were not allowed to use the wheels of their trade on this day.

Apples and pears had been stored in barns and attics, and meat was pickled and salted for the coming winter. Great sides of beef and bacon were hung to smoke in the chimney, and the new season's ale was drunk.

December

St. Nicholas's Day

December 6. The story is told that long ago, in another
country, a wicked landlord killed two young boys staying at
his inn, so that he could steal their possessions. He cut up
their bodies and put the pieces in a pickling tub. But the
Saint, Nicholas, had a vision of the murder, and he prayed
that the landlord might repent and the boys be restored to
life. His prayers were granted, and the boys sprang out of the
tub alive and well.

On this day mothers and fathers used to hide small gifts for
their children to find, to celebrate the patron saint of children.

Christmas Eve

December 24. On the first Christmas Eve nearly two thousand years ago, the baby Jesus was born in Bethlehem. He was born in a stable because there was no room for his mother Mary in the inn.

On this night animals and men can speak to each other and understand what the other says. On this night an extra bright star shines in the sky.

December 24. On the night before Christmas, children hang up their stockings, knowing that in the night Father Christmas will come and fill them with presents. There are mysterious parcels piled high under the Christmas Tree, and the house is full of secrets. Everything is waiting for Christmas Day.

Christmas Day

Christmas comes but once a year
But when it comes it brings good cheer.

December 25. On Christmas morning, children find treasures in their stockings. Everyone gives presents to everyone else. There is a Christmas feast with stuffed turkey and a plum pudding full of silver charms and coins. As they bite into their mince pies everyone makes a wish. Afterwards there are games like "The Farmer's in his Den" and "Blind Man's Buff".

New Year's Eve

December 31. On New Year's Eve we all wish each other good fortune for the coming year. In Scotland and Northern England, as soon as the midnight chimes have struck, we open the front door and wait for "the first footer", the first person to enter the house in the New Year. We shall be most fortunate if this is a young man, dark and handsome, carrying an evergreen branch. Before he speaks, he will lay a piece of coal on the fire, then give us a gift of food or money, and we shall welcome him, for he will bring us luck for the New Year.

Epilogue

It was when I saw Jenny Rhodes' illustrations of the flowers and local country customs of the seasons of the year, that I realised what an unsuspected number of these festivals were taking place throughout Britain today. Like everyone else, I knew about Pancake Day, Midsummer fires and Hallowe'en; but I'd never heard of egg rolling, I didn't know that the sun dances for joy on Easter day, or that geese used to be given shoes for the long march across the Midlands to the autumnal Goose Fair in Nottingham.

I first read the modern folklorists: Christina Hole, Mary Baker, Katherine Briggs, E. O. James, George Long and many others. Then I went back to Brand's *Observations on Antiquities*, a scholarly, well-documented work first published in 1795; an invaluable book of reference. I also read diaries, essays and novels of the last three centuries to try to catch the flavour of the ceremonies from writers who had personally witnessed and taken part in them.

I found, as I read, that a sort of pattern emerged. The picture is dominated by the four great seasonal feasts, to which a religious significance has been attached from the earliest times; Easter—the Spring festival, when the earth is re-born; Midsummer—when the sun is at its most powerful; Harvest—the gathering in of the crops; and Christmas, mid-winter—when the earth begins to turn again towards the sun. Around these, and less universal, are more regional observances connected with sowing of seed or preserving food against the lean winter months, like the Wassailing of the apple tree in January or Martinmas in November.

As well as such all-important ceremonies to ensure the well-being of the earth, there are scattered individual feasts in different parts of the British Isles. Some are to mark time-honoured rites, like Swan-Upping in July; others commemorate some particular historical event, like Plague Sunday in Eyam, and Bonfire Night. The difficulty has been to choose just thirty-three which would indicate these rich traditions—religious and historical—incorporating the hopes and fears of ordinary people, on which, perhaps more than we suspect, our life today is founded.

CATHERINE STORR

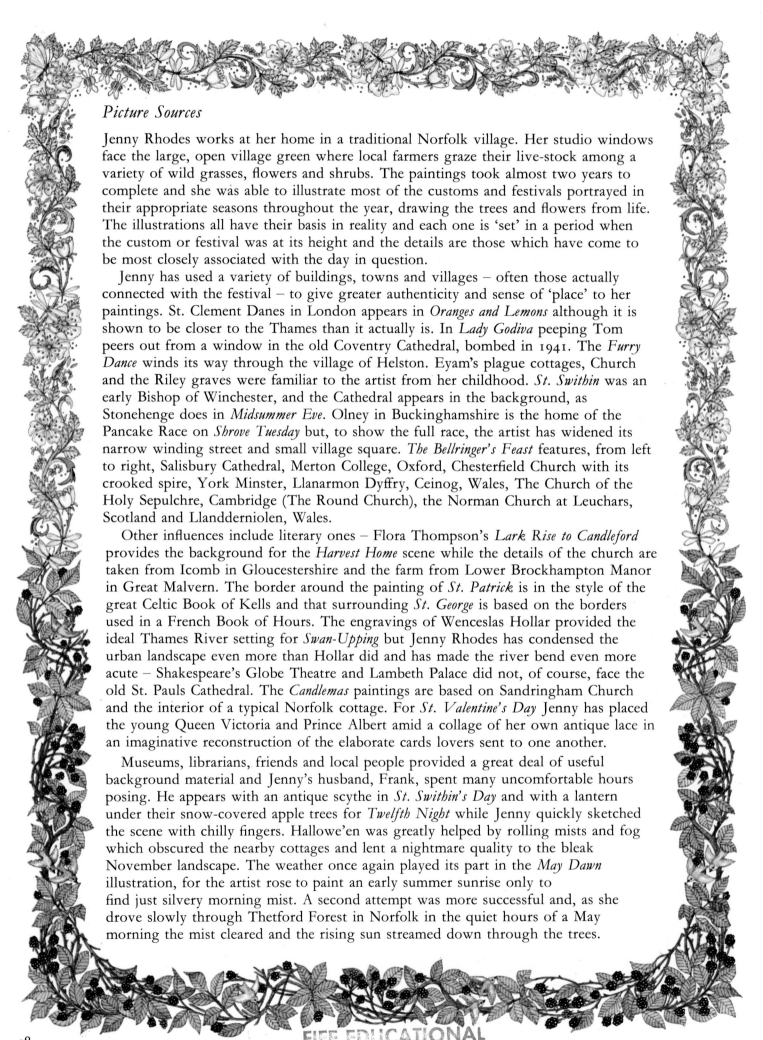

Picture Sources

Jenny Rhodes works at her home in a traditional Norfolk village. Her studio windows face the large, open village green where local farmers graze their live-stock among a variety of wild grasses, flowers and shrubs. The paintings took almost two years to complete and she was able to illustrate most of the customs and festivals portrayed in their appropriate seasons throughout the year, drawing the trees and flowers from life. The illustrations all have their basis in reality and each one is 'set' in a period when the custom or festival was at its height and the details are those which have come to be most closely associated with the day in question.

Jenny has used a variety of buildings, towns and villages – often those actually connected with the festival – to give greater authenticity and sense of 'place' to her paintings. St. Clement Danes in London appears in *Oranges and Lemons* although it is shown to be closer to the Thames than it actually is. In *Lady Godiva* peeping Tom peers out from a window in the old Coventry Cathedral, bombed in 1941. The *Furry Dance* winds its way through the village of Helston. Eyam's plague cottages, Church and the Riley graves were familiar to the artist from her childhood. *St. Swithin* was an early Bishop of Winchester, and the Cathedral appears in the background, as Stonehenge does in *Midsummer Eve*. Olney in Buckinghamshire is the home of the Pancake Race on *Shrove Tuesday* but, to show the full race, the artist has widened its narrow winding street and small village square. *The Bellringer's Feast* features, from left to right, Salisbury Cathedral, Merton College, Oxford, Chesterfield Church with its crooked spire, York Minster, Llanarmon Dyffry, Ceinog, Wales, The Church of the Holy Sepulchre, Cambridge (The Round Church), the Norman Church at Leuchars, Scotland and Llandderniolen, Wales.

Other influences include literary ones – Flora Thompson's *Lark Rise to Candleford* provides the background for the *Harvest Home* scene while the details of the church are taken from Icomb in Gloucestershire and the farm from Lower Brockhampton Manor in Great Malvern. The border around the painting of *St. Patrick* is in the style of the great Celtic Book of Kells and that surrounding *St. George* is based on the borders used in a French Book of Hours. The engravings of Wenceslas Hollar provided the ideal Thames River setting for *Swan-Upping* but Jenny Rhodes has condensed the urban landscape even more than Hollar did and has made the river bend even more acute – Shakespeare's Globe Theatre and Lambeth Palace did not, of course, face the old St. Pauls Cathedral. The *Candlemas* paintings are based on Sandringham Church and the interior of a typical Norfolk cottage. For *St. Valentine's Day* Jenny has placed the young Queen Victoria and Prince Albert amid a collage of her own antique lace in an imaginative reconstruction of the elaborate cards lovers sent to one another.

Museums, librarians, friends and local people provided a great deal of useful background material and Jenny's husband, Frank, spent many uncomfortable hours posing. He appears with an antique scythe in *St. Swithin's Day* and with a lantern under their snow-covered apple trees for *Twelfth Night* while Jenny quickly sketched the scene with chilly fingers. Hallowe'en was greatly helped by rolling mists and fog which obscured the nearby cottages and lent a nightmare quality to the bleak November landscape. The weather once again played its part in the *May Dawn* illustration, for the artist rose to paint an early summer sunrise only to find just silvery morning mist. A second attempt was more successful and, as she drove slowly through Thetford Forest in Norfolk in the quiet hours of a May morning the mist cleared and the rising sun streamed down through the trees.